CHARACTER

Character—distinctive qualities: the set of qualities that make somebody or something distinctive, especially somebody's qualities of mind and feeling[1]

Most people enjoy pie or cake, or both. There are so many varieties it would take up an entire page just to list them. In fact, even within types of pie (for example, cherry) and cake (for example, chocolate) there are numerous varieties and styles. Each one is made up of many ingredients that give the pie or cake a particular taste. The parts make up the whole.

In some ways, people are like pie and cake. Our human ingredients (character traits) make up the whole of our being as reflected in our speech and actions. They are, in essence, who we are and determine how we are viewed by others. Our thoughts, feelings, and expressions of purity, honesty, work, love, servanthood, and so on, are revealed in the things we say and do. In turn, our words and actions give off an aroma and a taste that informs others about who we are as a person. Our goal should be that our lives would be a pleasing fragrance not only to God but to those we encounter as well.

During the next six weeks, you will learn how to develop healthy character within your teenager. Our prayer is that, at the end of this study, you will have discovered ways to build upon the character already developing within your teen. May God bless you on this journey of discovery.

1. http://www.bing.com/Dictionary/search?q=define+character&FORM=DTPDIA&qpvt=character+definition Accessed March 9, 2011.

HOW TO GET THE MOST FROM THIS STUDY

For any study to be effective, it must be functional. In other words, you must be able to get something out of it that is beneficial to you. This study is designed to be practical and is written in such a way that you can apply the principles contained within its pages the very day you read them. This study is created to be done over a six-week period. The topics include:

Purity: Television, movies, the Internet, etc., make it difficult for teenagers to develop pure hearts and minds. This study will help you understand the importance of purity and the ways you can help your teen develop a pure lifestyle.

Servanthood: We live in a "me" world that focuses on self. Teenagers need to understand God's call to be servants. This study will help you understand how to develop a servanthood mentality within your teenager.

Loving Others: What does it mean to love others as Christ does? This study will help you understand how you can help your teenager develop a love for others in both thought and action.

Integrity: Honesty and transparency are rare in our world. Cheating and the acceptance of white lies run rampant in teen culture. This study will help you develop a view and lifestyle of honesty and authenticity within your teenager.

Work Ethic: Work is a part of life. However, not everyone has the same view and attitude toward work. This study will help you develop a sense of hard work and discipline within your teenager.

Spiritual Sensitivity: Each day teens are bombarded by all kinds of messages and voices. It can be tough to distinguish which ones are worth listening to. This study will help you develop sensitivity to the things of God within your teenager.

Each weekly study contains the following:

- **Parent Article.** Each week's study begins with an article that examines the topic for that week. These articles are written with you in mind, for the purpose of helping you better understand the theme you will explore that particular week. Take your time as you read, allowing for reflection on its message. You may consider reading it more than once. Each article concludes with tips to help you better understand and develop healthy character within your teenager.
- **Character Practices.** At the end of each article, there is a section dedicated to helping you apply the week's theme. There are three separate ways we provide you opportunities to practice: as a parent, as a couple, and as a family. Whether you are a married couple, single parent, blended family, or have more than one teenager, you choose which practices are most conducive to your family situation. This is not homework but a way to help you grow as individuals and as a family.
- **Family Devotional Guide.** We have provided a five-day devotional guide aimed at helping your family begin to think about Scripture, talk about its meaning, and spend time in prayer together. These are just discussion starters. Take as much time as you need to talk and pray.
- **Leader's Guide.** If you would like to use this as a small-group resource, there is a leader's guide located at the back.

PURITY

Purity isn't a word we hear much anymore. Do you remember the tagline for Ivory soap? *Ivory is 99.44% pure.* I always wondered why they just didn't go for 100 percent. Probably because, if they advertised that their product was 100% pure, no one would believe them.

We live in a world that is extremely skeptical of anything labeled *pure*. However, we can't deny that Jesus said, "Blessed are the pure in heart" (Matthew 5:8); and Paul wrote to Timothy, "Keep yourself pure" (1 Timothy 5:22). Even King David sang, "Create in me a pure heart" (Psalm 51:10).

It could be from David's song that we get our best idea of what it means to desire to be pure. David shares these words after having an adulterous affair with Bathsheba and orchestrating the death of her husband. Seeking purity is not asking to be perfect. It is a perfecting—a purification, if you will—of our motives.

The obvious question is, how does a teen (or anyone, for that matter) keep a pure heart and a clean mind in such an impure and dirty world? The power of television, movies, music, and the Internet have incredible influence on the thinking and behavior of young people. Teens watch four hours of screen media each day, listen to two hours of media each day, and when you add in what little teens read each day, they are saturated with 44.5 hours of media each week. Upon graduation from high school, teens will have watched 23,000 hours of television. The average teen spends 16.7 hours per week online, navigating the worldwide web's more than 40 million websites, 12% of which are pornographic. (It's been said that 70% of all pornography produced eventually finds its way to teenagers.)

The temptation might be to eliminate all media from the house, but not many families would want to give up the obvious benefits of modern technology. However, there are things parents can do to modify or nullify the harmful effects of unbridled media.

So what's a family to do? In regard to television, limits should be set and agreed upon as to how much TV is enough each day. Let teens tell you what program or programs are worth watching and why. Occasionally watch their programs with them. Talk about the overall message and how the message matches up with biblical values. Talk about the possibility of your family going on a TV diet—that is, going a day, a week, or maybe even a month without watching television. Maybe you select a day each week when the family reads together, plays together, or works on a hobby together. I know we live in an age when homes have a television in almost every room, but television in the children's bedroom is a temptation that doesn't need to happen.

We've come a long way from the days of labeling all movies as evil and a tool of the devil. We now believe that Christians are able to discern whether a movie is acceptable or not by judging its content. The movie rating system helps some but is not always dependable in conveying what we as parents would consider appropriate. Of course, we're against gratuitous sex and violence, but sometimes storylines in PG and PG-13 movies have content we are uncomfortable with. Parents should take advantage of family and Christian websites that give extensive details on every movie out today. Let your kids know that you will be asking them about what they've seen—not as a watchdog but because you want to train them to think through Christian filters about what they see and hear.

For teens, music is more than mere entertainment or a diversion from the stress of life; it is the language of their culture. Not being a lyrics person myself, there is little I can understand about today's music. Most teens I talk to understand clearly the messages of the songs to which they are listening. Their music reflects their beliefs, or at least shows us the things they tolerate. Their listening habits also reflect an acceptance of the lifestyle of the artists performing the music. When the discussion about the lyrics happens, there should also be discussion about what the artists stand for.

For teens, music is more than mere entertainment or a diversion from the stress of life; it is the language of their culture.

The Internet might be the single greatest problem in the battle for the hearts and minds of your children. The amount of time some spend on the computer borders on addiction and certainly opens up a myriad of negative possibilities. Many suggest the use of a filter on the family computer, and there are number of good ones. The downside is that most computer-savvy teens can work around filters or find computers without them. Also, the filter sometimes eliminates things that are okay and information you really need. And most importantly, a filter doesn't help teach teens how to think for themselves about what is right or wrong. As a parent, I would use a filter only after discussing it with my kids, and then we would set up some agreed-upon guidelines, such as:

1. A time limit is in effect unless it's a research project.
2. No personal information is to be given out.
3. Adding new social networking contacts should be run by the parents first.
4. Parents should be added to the friends list of any social media sites.
5. All inappropriate communications, such as anything pornographic or bullying, should be reported to Mom or Dad.

PARENT TIPS

1. ***Set*** a regular time each week to discuss what your teens are watching and listening to.
2. ***Familiarize*** yourself not only with the music your teens are listening to but also with the artists who sing the music.
3. ***Don't be*** too concerned with fads. By design, they are here today and gone tomorrow and usually reflect young people's need for identity.
4. ***Make sure*** your teens understand that computer filters and censors are in not in place because you do not trust them but are a protection from unscrupulous predators they would never suspect.
5. ***Teens should*** understand that purity is not perfection but a standard of honesty and morals that would be beyond reproach.

Character Practices

For the Parent

- What is your concept of what it means to be pure? Do you feel that purity is realistic in the society you are a part of?
- Think about the movies you watched, the music you listened to, and the television programs you tuned into as a teenager. How did these things have an impact on you then, and now?
- How familiar and aware are you with and of the things your teenager listens to and watches?
- Think about your lifestyle. What kind of example are you setting when it comes to music, movies, and television?

For the Couple

- Share with each other how satisfied you are about the listening and watching habits of your family.
- Discuss your current strategy for helping build an atmosphere of purity within your home. What needs to change?
- Are you satisfied with the amount of time you spend talking with your teenager about the importance of developing a pure heart and mind?
- Talk about ways you can become more familiar with the listening and viewing habits of your teen. Be sure these are healthy and positive methods.

For the Family

- Take time this week to watch a movie as a family. Make sure it is a movie everyone agrees on. Before the movie, ask everyone to think about the positive and negative messages of the movie. After the movie, take time for everyone to share their thoughts and feelings.
- Set aside time this week to share with each other your favorite song, movie, and television program. Be sure each person feels free to share openly.
- Challenge everyone in the family—including yourself—to become more aware of the messages they receive from music and television.

Monday—Read 1 Timothy 1:1-11.

Begin to Think: Paul warns Timothy about false teachers. There are those who preach a different belief from Paul's. He urges Timothy to deal with these teachers of false doctrine because their teachings are contrary to sound doctrine—the true gospel of Jesus.

Begin to Talk: Why is following sound doctrine important? How can people lead us astray with false teaching?

Begin to Pray: That God would give you a discerning spirit when it comes to his truth.

Tuesday—Read 1 Timothy 2:1-6.

Begin to Think: When Paul writes this letter, Nero is the leader of Rome. In these verses, he says the church should pray for everyone, including the king and the government. In light of the persecution the Christians face during this time, prayer could bring about peace and the salvation of those who do not believe in Christ.

Begin to Talk: Why should we pray for our government leaders? Why should we pray for the salvation of others?

Begin to Pray: For someone you know who is not a follower of Christ.

Wednesday—Read 1 Timothy 3:1-16.

Begin to Think: Paul gives Timothy the prerequisites needed for those who wish to be leaders in the church. However, these are good characteristics for any Christian. All Christians should strive to live out these qualities.

Begin to Talk: Who are the leaders in the church? Why should everyone exemplify the characteristics Paul lists in these verses?

Begin to Pray: That you would live by the light of his Spirit.

Thursday—Read 1 Timothy 4:1-16.

Begin to Think: False teaching distorts the truth of God. Paul warns Timothy not to have anything to do with this kind of teaching. He tells Timothy to command and teach God's truth and to set an example for all believers.

Begin to Talk: How can we spot false teaching? Why should we set an example for others to follow?

Begin to Pray: That your life would be a godly example to others.

Friday—Read 1 Timothy 6:3-15.

Begin to Think: In this final chapter of 1 Timothy, Paul warns Timothy not to be like the false teachers who seek financial gain. Rather, he should pursue righteousness, godliness, faith, love, endurance, and gentleness. As followers of Christ, these are things we should pursue as well.

Begin to Talk: What should our motive be for following Christ? How are some of the ways we can pursue righteousness, godliness, faith, love, endurance, and gentleness?

Begin to Pray: That your life would be a living testimony of God's truth.

SERVANTHOOD

Think about this: *Do teenagers learn servanthood by practicing being a servant, or do they learn about being a servant and then go out to practice servanthood?* I know many wonder which comes first, the head knowledge or the actual doing. After so many years in youth ministry, I'm convinced the knowledge and the doing go hand in hand. You don't want to wait until your son or daughter understands everything there is to know about human need for them to be involved is some kind of mission effort. On the other hand, every mission project should involve some kind of intellectual processing. One person described missions as a heart, head, and hands process—involving the emotions, the intellect, and the actual doing. That makes all kinds of sense to me.

Missions and servanthood are not a hard sell for today's teenager. Most are looking to be involved in worthwhile projects that are bigger than themselves. The fact that it is both biblical and Christlike is icing on the cake. In a room in Jerusalem, the disciples were arguing about what titles and positions they might have after Jesus overthrew the Roman Empire and restored the Jews to their rightful place of authority. As they argued, Jesus took a towel and wrapped it around his waist. Then he took a basin of water and began washing their feet. The message was clear then and now: If you want to change the world, you must first become a servant. So how do teens learn to be servants? The best way is that they hear it taught and see it lived out at home.

After my parents' divorce, my mom prayed that God would allow her to buy a new car. She saved and borrowed and finally had enough to buy a brand-new vehicle. Within weeks of getting that car, my mother told the Sunday school superintendent that God had allowed her to have that car, but it was really his. In light of this, every Sunday morning, we picked up kids for Sunday school who needed a ride to church. I learned early on from my mom the concept of servanthood.

Hopefully servanthood for your family isn't just writing a big check to the church or going on an exciting mission trip to Costa Rica, though either one or both could be God's plan for you. What I hope would happen in the servant training process is not just the act of kindness but an understanding of why we do the act. The entire family should understand that the giving of a tithe is not just our spiritual obligation but an opportunity to be servants with the financial blessings God has given us. The same is true for the building pledge and our missions offering. With so many needs around the world, not everyone will go to the mission field. But if we give the equivalent of a day's, week's, or month's salary for missions, it's like actually giving a part of our lives to make it possible for someone to go in our place.

Your teens should understand that your serving on the church board, preparing meals for funerals, teaching Sunday school, or planting flowers on church workdays are all gifts of love that constitute a servant's heart. These are not seen as intrusions on your time, and if they are, please stop doing them. Parents and church leaders must be careful about walking that fine line that takes them away from home too many nights and hinders their relationships with their families. Teens should understand why you do these things for all the right reasons and, in the process, learn the concept of servanthood. As I understand it, stewardship is taking the gifts and resources given to us by God and giving them back in a way that helps build his kingdom on earth. This is the essence of servanthood.

Stewardship is taking the gifts and resources given to us by God and giving them back in a way that helps build his kingdom on earth.

If you are fortunate enough as a family to do a missions experience together, whether it be a visit to a local soup kitchen or food bank, or going halfway around the world to a mission station, allow your teen to discover the blessing of seeing God work in his own way among people unlike themsleves.

None of these experiences are about your family seeing how much better off they are than other people. This is often the reaction of the more immature. It's not even about counting the many material blessings that have been bestowed on you and your family, though this is often a natural response. It is about rejoicing that God meets people at their point of need and uses us in the process. To see people existing in a standard of living that would make your kids miserable—yet these people are happy in Jesus—is an eye-opening experience that I covet for all teens.

The key is, you don't have to wait for your teen's maturity to kick in before you start talking about and doing service projects. God will use the experience for his glory at whatever developmental level your teen may be.

PARENT TIPS

1. ***On the list*** of things you discuss as a family on a regular basis should be your stewardship of all resources.
2. ***One of the best*** things you can do as a family in the area of servanthood is support a child from Nazarene Compassionate Ministries. For about $25 a month, you and your family can feed and educate a child from a majority-world country and keep in regular contact with him or her.
3. ***Don't be discouraged*** if your teen doesn't get every lesson that could be learned from a service project. In God's good timing, he will use your teen's availability as a learning tool.
4. ***Don't forget*** to give God verbal credit in front of your children for what he has done.
5. ***It's a given*** that there are a number of things you do as a parent that are taken for granted. There are probably things teens do that go unmentioned too. It wouldn't be a bad idea to have a time to look each other in the face and say thank you for specific acts of love and service in the home.

Character Practices

For the Parent

- Think about the word *servanthood.* What images come to mind? What emotions are evoked within you?
- During your teen years, did you do anything that would fall into the category of servanthood? How did you feel about those experiences?
- As an adult, what are the ways you practice servanthood? How do you feel about these experiences?
- Reflect on the ways you foster a servant spirit in the life of your teenager. What things would you like to see happen in the future?

For the Couple

- Share with each other your concepts of servanthood.
- Take time to talk about whether service to others is a high priority in your family. If it is not, discuss why this is the case.
- Discuss the ways in which you nurture servanthood within your family.
- Talk with each other about the ways you would like to see your family become more others oriented.

For the Family

- Think about one act of service you could do as a family within the next few weeks. Then create plan to carry out this act.
- Talk to your pastor and ask if there is an act of service your family could be involved in at your church or in your church community. This might be cleaning an elderly person's yard, helping out at a food bank, or volunteering at a homeless shelter.
- Watch the movie *End of the Spear.* This is a movie about the difference our lives can make. Afterwards, take time to discuss the thoughts and feelings each family member had during the movie.

Monday—Read 2 Timothy 1:3-18.

Begin to Think: Paul is a mentor to Timothy. They have worked together and parted ways. In these verses, Paul acknowledges Timothy's faith and the faith of his mother and grandmother. He encourages Timothy to keep living in the spirit of power, love, and self-discipline.

Begin to Talk: How do power, love, and self-discipline work in the Christian life? What are ways we can strengthen our faith in God?

Begin to Pray: That God would fill your life with his joy.

Tuesday—Read 2 Timothy 2:1-13.

Begin to Think: Paul uses the soldier, farmer, and athlete to describe our experience serving God. These show us what is involved in working hard and staying faithful to God for the long haul.

Begin to Talk: How is our relationship with God like that of a soldier, farmer, and athlete? What is the reward for those who remain faithful to God?

Begin to Pray: That you would serve God wholeheartedly.

Wednesday—Read 2 Timothy 2:14-26.

Begin to Think: The things we say are important. However, our actions will speak louder than our words. Paul reminds Timothy that his godly actions will reinforce his teachings within the church. More times than not, our actions carry more weight than our words.

Begin to Talk: What are the ways we can flee evil desires? How do our actions affect those around us?

Begin to Pray: That you would be kind to everyone through the power of God's Spirit.

Thursday—Read 2 Timothy 3:1-16.

Begin to Think: Paul gives Timothy an idea of what life will be like in the days prior to Christ's second coming. Although he is talking about the future, Paul tells Timothy not to be influenced by those who currently practice godlessness. In the end, these people will not succeed.

Begin to Talk: How do we avoid the negative influence of others? What are the benefits of God's Word to the life of the Christian?

Begin to Pray: That you would allow God's Word to change your life.

Friday—Read 2 Timothy 4:1-8.

Begin to Think: The Bible is God's Word. Paul tells Timothy to preach this Word. The Word will help guard against false teachings and be a guide for people's lives. Paul tells Timothy to remain faithful through hardships because God will reward those who stray true to him.

Begin to Talk: How does someone who is not a pastor preach the Word? What is the "good fight" Paul is talking about?

Begin to Pray: That God would help you stay faithful during both easy and difficult times.

In the last chapter of John's gospel, Jesus confronts his friend Peter in a resurrection appearance on the shore of the Sea of Galilee. Jesus asks Peter a very important question (John 21:15): "Simon, son of John, do you truly love me more than these?"

The Greek word Jesus uses for the word *love* is *agape*. Those of us who have grown up in the church have heard sermons and lessons on *agape* love all our lives. *Agape* is unconditional love, no strings attached. It's like saying, "The ribcage of my life is pulled back, and you can say or do anything you want. It will not change my commitment or devotion to you." We are familiar with the word today; yet in Jesus' day, it was a word seldom used, mainly because it didn't fit into the culture. People loved out of respect or loyalty. A person loved because he owed it to another person, but to love just to love was unheard of.

One could say that the life of Jesus literally defined the word *agape*. It is probably because of his unfamiliarity with the word, or the commitment that goes with it, that Peter is only able to respond, "Yes, Lord, you know that I love you."

The correct English translation of the word Peter uses is love, but Peter actually answers with an entirely different Greek word, *phileo*. *Phileo* is a family type of love; loving that we share things in common, like the family name. The fellowship we have at church reflects this *phileo* love.

Peter is giving back to Jesus the only kind of love he understands. He is telling him, "Jesus, until I saw you crucified, I was with you all the way. I love the things you do, the things you say, and I believe we have a common mission to change the world." But Peter doesn't get the *agape* aspect. This kind of love would require him to surrender his own personal agenda and expectations in order for him to change the world as Christ would change it, without swords or political maneuvering.

It's this *agape* love that Paul talks about in Ephesians 5:25 when he says, "Husbands, love your wives, just as Christ loved the church and gave himself up for her." It is *agape* love, Paul says, that is patient and kind. This love "does not envy, it does not boast, it is not proud. It is not rude, it is not self-seeking, it is not easily angered, it keeps no record of wrongs. Love does not delight in evil but rejoices with the truth. It always protects, always trusts, always hopes, always perseveres" (1 Corinthians 13:4-6). Just like Jesus' teaching, Paul is not making a list of things people should do to be loving. Instead, Paul is sharing what people become when the love of Christ transforms them from the inside out. He's saying that if you want a lesson on how to love others, come to an understanding of just how much Jesus loves you.

Dallas Willard in his book *The Divine Conspiracy* writes that Jesus illustrates the concept of *agape* love throughout his Sermon on the Mount. Take, for instance, Matthew 7:1, "Do not judge, or you too will be judged." Willard suggests that judging often leads to blaming and condemning, which usually lead to anger and broken relationships. Condemnation reflects a person's value or worth, so when someone makes a judgment against someone else in the family, the hurt can run deep and often feels irreparable. If Paul is right when he says real love believes the best and hopes for the best, then nothing will convince your teen that you love him or her more than the knowledge that you believe he or she wants to do the right thing, unless you see proof to the contrary.

***Agape* is unconditional love, no strings attached.**

As a parent, it will usually fall on you to make judgment calls about behavior when the need arises. Nevertheless, making any correction should be done with genuine love. Discipline isn't easy, so both the parent and teen should know that love hurts. That's why any confrontation is not a matter of "straightening someone out;" instead, it is an effort at restoration and reconciliation. Just pounding on someone verbally about the wrongness of their actions does little to bring about healing, let alone demonstrate Christlike love.

Perhaps the best way to show God's love for others is to remember that those you are tempted to judge have done things you also may have done. Willard writes, "This totally removes any sense of self-righteousness or superiority, which, if it is present, will certainly make restoration impossible."[2] The key to understanding *agape* love is learning to live life with an uncondemning spirit that reflects Christ.

2. Willard, Dallas. *The Divine Conspiracy* (New York: HarperCollins Publishers, 1998), p. 219.

PARENT TIPS

1. ***True love*** allows parents to say "forgive me" when they are wrong. Don't hesitate to go further than saying you're sorry; ask to be forgiven.
2. ***Love involves*** eye contact and touching. Even if you are not a "touchy-feely" family, looking at your daughter when you talk to her and touching your son's shoulder as you pass by add points to your teen's emotional bank.
3. ***Your teens*** should hear how you've had to learn to love some seemingly unlovable people and what God has taught you about loving others.
4. ***A good exercise*** for your family would be to choose a people group you really don't know much about and maybe don't appreciate. The idea is to find information on this group, to discover what life is like for them, to understand how they think, and to learn why they do what they do.
5. ***Life is uncertain.*** Decide as a family that the last thing you will hear each other say as you say goodnight at bedtime is "I love you."

Character Practices

For the Parent

- Think about your teen years. Who expressed (through words and actions) a loving attitude toward you? How did they impact your life?
- Take time to think about all the ways you show love to your family. How do your actions impact each person?
- Reflect on all the ways that your family shows love toward you. How do their actions have an effect on your life?
- Consider one way you can express love toward your teenager this week.

For the Couple

- Share with each other the ways you as parents can express love toward your teenager.
- Discuss how you as a couple model for your family loving attitudes toward each other.
- Talk with each other about the ways you can foster within your teenager a loving attitude toward your family and others.
- Take time to evaluate the way you talk about and treat others outside your family. How might the things you say and do impact your teenager?

For the Family

- Challenge each person in the family to do at least one selfless act for someone outside your household during the next two weeks.
- Decide as a family to say "I love you" to each other more often.
- Look for opportunities to talk about ways each member could intentionally express love toward those outside your family.

FAMILY DEVOTIONAL GUIDE

Monday—Read John 14:1-4.

Begin to Think: Jesus has just told his disciples that he is going away. Upon hearing this, the disciples are distraught. Jesus gives them words of encouragement and hope. The key for them is to trust in the words of Jesus. The key for us is to trust in the words of Jesus.

Begin to Talk: What are some of the troubles we face in life? How do these words of Jesus give us hope?

Begin to Pray: That you would place your full trust in Jesus.

Tuesday—Read John 14:5-14.

Begin to Think: Thomas asks Jesus where he is going and how they can know the way. Jesus replies that he *is* the way. Jesus means that he is the way to a relationship with the Father; he is the truth of God and gives life now and eternally.

Begin to Talk: What does it mean that Jesus is "the way, the truth, and the life"? How do we have the faith Jesus mentions in verse 12?

Begin to Pray: That you would follow the way, live in the truth, and accept the life Jesus offers.

Wednesday—Read John 14:15-30.

Begin to Think: Jesus will be leaving the earth physically. However, he will not leave his disciples alone. Jesus says he will send the Holy Spirit. If we allow, the Spirit will live within us, guide, direct, convict, counsel, teach, and bring glory to Christ through our lives.

Begin to Talk: How does our obedience to Christ's commands show our love for him? Why is reliance on the Holy Spirit so important to our Christian life?

Begin to Pray: That you would allow the presence of the Holy Spirit to saturate your life.

Thursday—Read John 15:1-17.

Begin to Think: Jesus is the vine, we are the branches, and God is the gardener. We must stay connected to the life-giving branch and bear fruit. God prunes those who bear fruit so that more fruit can be produced. The keys for the branches are to stay connected to the vine and to allow the gardener to prune us.

Begin to Talk: What does it mean to bear fruit? How do we remain connected to the "true vine"?

Begin to Pray: That you abide in Christ and that his Word would abide in you.

Friday—Read John 15:18-27.

Begin to Think: Jesus tells the disciples that the world may hate them because of their relationship with him. The disciples will face the same hatred and persecution from the world as Christ has. Yet they can take comfort in knowing they will have the power of the Holy Spirit working in their lives.

Begin to Talk: What does it mean to be hated and persecuted for your faith in Jesus? How does this help us during times of persecution?

Begin to Pray: That you would rely on the power of the Holy Spirit.

INTEGRITY

Jesus had some things to say about integrity. From Matthew 5:33, 37:

> You have heard that it was said to the people long ago, "Do not break your oath, but keep the oaths you have made to the Lord." But I tell you . . . simply let your "Yes" be "Yes," and your "No," "No;" anything beyond this comes from the evil one.

This is not Jesus' anti-cursing speech. It doesn't even come under the "Do not take the Lord's name in vain" prohibition. This lesson is about telling the truth. The question was, how will people know when we are really telling the truth and not lying to them?

Lying was a problem in Jesus' day, and being told the truth was important to most in the Jewish culture. So to ensure that what they were saying was true, they took oaths, much like we would say, "I cross my heart." In their culture, words meant something. So if they swore to God or made an oath in God's name, it indicated the seriousness of their words. As often happened, Jewish religious leaders were always looking for the right words, the right actions, and the correct techniques to look and sound religious. They were content to rank various oaths so people would judge their character by the words they used.

Jesus cuts to the heart of the matter. Do not swear by the Lord, or the heavens, or the earth, or anything on the earth. You are who you are. People should be able to judge your character and the truthfulness of your words by the way you live your life, pure and simple.

A few years ago, I was staying at a hotel in Dallas when I felt the need for a diet soda. I made my way down to the end of the hallway, where the vending machines were, and dropped in a quarter. The quarter funneled through the machine, made some sounds, and came out the coin return. Thinking I had used a faulty 25-cent piece, I put another quarter in the slot. Once again I got the same sounds, and the coin returned. I tried another quarter. I got the sounds, and the quarter returned, but this time a can of soda popped out. I thought this was really strange, so I tried it again. Three quarters in, three quarters returned, and after the third quarter, a can of soda appeared. I was so fascinated with the way this machine operated that I got two more cans. For the first time in my life, it seemed I had found a soda machine that didn't care whether I paid for the can; it just wanted to know I had the ability to pay.

Of course, I knew there was probably a real person somewhere who did care whether I paid for the product, and I had to make things right. The next day, when checking out, I handed the clerk three dollars. "What's this for?" she asked.

"Well," I said, "you have an extra-generous soda machine on the sixth floor that gave me four cans of soda yesterday. The machine wouldn't take my money, but someone is expecting me to pay for those cans, so I'm leaving the money with you."

I'm not trying to set myself up as the prime example of honesty and integrity, but I do believe one's character of integrity is best displayed when no one is looking or seems to care. The salesman who says to me, "Mr. Sivewright, I have to be honest with you. That hat you are about to purchase makes you look like a goof" might be doing me a favor. But he also knows that if I buy the hat and wear it in front of my friends, who start laughing hysterically, I'll never buy from him again. He has a vested interest in telling me the truth. It's one thing to tell the truth because it's good business. It's another thing to tell the truth because it's a matter of character. I don't mean brutal truth telling, like, "That dress really makes you look fat;" or, "You drive like a maniac." As true as those statements might be, there are kinder and gentler ways to tell people what they need to know.

Most important is that you as parents be known as people who keep your word and stick to your commitments.

Most important is that you as parents be known as people who keep your word and stick to your commitments. People of integrity don't break promises and can be counted on to be where they say they will be when they say they will be there. Don't think your teens haven't noticed these characteristics about you. The tragedy for this generation is that they have learned from society that truth just doesn't matter.

My generation thought of lying primarily as a way to gain unfair advantage. Advantage doesn't matter as much to your teen. It's just that truth is relative for them. If politicians make promises they have no intention of keeping just to win an election, it really doesn't matter to the current generation because they don't expect politicians to tell the truth anyway. The same goes for television commercials and subjects at school. Tell me this cream will wipe out all my pimples, and it doesn't? It's okay. Tell me God had nothing to do with the creation of the world? No big deal.

Parents need to explain and model for their teens that honesty and integrity are the foundation of relationships. Without them, love doesn't have much of a chance, and everybody wants to be loved.

PARENT TIPS

1. ***Explain*** to your teens that half-truths are as good as lies because they lead a person to assume something that is not true.
2. ***Be honest*** with your speech. If "I'll do my best" or "Let me think about it" have become code words for "I probably won't" or "No," then just say what you're really thinking and why.
3. ***Your teens*** need to know that you'll love them even if they lie to you, but they also need to know that there are consequences for their actions.
4. ***Just for fun,*** ask your teens if they think it is ever right to lie and see how they answer. As a parent, you really need to know what they're thinking about telling the truth.
5. ***It wouldn't*** be a bad idea to develop a family covenant of things each member of the family is committed to—whether it's never missing a sporting event or concert or eating breakfast together every Saturday morning.

Character Practices

For the Parent

- Think back to your teen years. How would you rate your honesty level?
- Think about your life now. How would you rate your honesty level?
- Consider your closest relationships. Are they lived out with honesty and integrity?
- Take time to think about your interaction with other people during the past week. Were you honest in your relationships? Were there any lies or half-truths?

For the Couple

- Share with each other your concepts of honesty and integrity.
- Discuss the honesty level of your home. Do you feel there is an atmosphere of openness and honesty?
- Talk about the ways you promote honesty within your home. Are there things you would like to see change? If so, what would it take to make those changes?
- Think about one thing you as a couple can do this week to set an example of honesty for your teen.

For the Family

- Look for an opportunity to have a conversation with your family about honesty. Consider what you will say beforehand.
- Discuss with your family ways that you can keep each other accountable when it comes practicing honesty and integrity.
- As a family, make a list of 5 things a person can do to be honest in his/her relationships. Have each person sign the list as a commitment to practice the things listed.

Monday—Read 1 Thessalonians 1:2-10.

Begin to Think: Paul begins this letter to the church at Thessalonica with a word of thanksgiving. He is thankful for their work, labor, and endurance. They are imitators of Jesus and are examples to other believers. They have turned from idols to the one true God, and their lives are making a difference.

Begin to Talk: If someone were to write a letter about your Christian life, what would they be thankful for? How can we be imitators of Jesus?

Begin to Pray: That the message of your life would make a difference in the lives of those around you.

Tuesday—Read 1 Thessalonians 2:1-16.

Begin to Think: Paul and Silas have been missionaries to the church but have fled the city due to an angry mob. Some in the city thought that their time there was a failure; however, their church was doing well, so their ministry was not in vain. In chapter 2, Paul describes the godly relationship he has with the church.

Begin to Talk: How do we foster godly relationships? What are ways you can encourage others in the faith?

Begin to Pray: That you would be an encouragement to those around you.

Wednesday—Read 1 Thessalonians 3:1-13.

Begin to Think: Paul does not return to the church but instead sends Timothy. When Timothy returns to Paul, he brings back a good report about his experience in Thessalonica. The church is known for its faith and love and for standing firm amidst distress and persecution.

Begin to Talk: What are the ways we can remain faithful during trials? How do we stand firm in the Lord?

Begin to Pray: That your love would increase and overflow.

Thursday—Read 1 Thessalonians 4:1-12.

Begin to Think: Paul gives the church instruction on how to live to please God. Our faith should be seen in every aspect of our lives. Inside and outside, we should reflect the presence of God. The call of God is for us to live holy lives through the power of his Spirit.

Begin to Talk: How do we please God? What does it mean to live a holy life?

Begin to Pray: That you may a live a holy life by the power of the Holy Spirit.

Friday—Read 1 Thessalonians 5:1-10.

Begin to Think: Paul ends his letter to the church with a warning to be ready for Jesus' return to earth. Christ came to earth, died, rose again, ascended to the right hand of the Father, and someday will return. Paul says the church should live prepared for his return.

Begin to Talk: What is the "day of the Lord"? How do we live every day in preparation for Christ's return?

Begin to Pray: That you would live alert and self-controlled.

WORK ETHIC

When I was a youth pastor I planned to take my seniors on a spring break mission trip to Guatemala. This was their first trip out of the United States as a group, and it was a huge deal. We practiced, we prayed, and we raised money for the trip. One day one of my teens came to me and said he wouldn't be able to go on the trip because he couldn't get off work. I thought this strange because he worked part time at the local shoe store that was owned by one of our church board members. Sure enough, the owner had explained to him that spring was the busiest season for selling shoes and he just couldn't afford to lose him for a week.

I'm sure our board member thought he was doing the student a favor by helping him understand the seriousness of responsibility in the workplace by telling him he would lose his job if he went to Guatemala, but the owner underestimated his commitment to the youth group and the mission trip.

There are some things I'd like to say about teenagers and work before we get to the topic of work ethic. Research says that only 1 in every 10 teenagers has to work in order to support his or her family. A majority of teens are doing jobs they don't necessarily enjoy and certainly do not see making careers of. There are some things to be gained by teenagers taking on part-time jobs, such as learning new skills, learning to manage money, learning to deal with the public, and learning to deal with authority figures other than their parents or teachers. I understand that if the alternative to working is sitting around watching television, parents will vote for work every time. But what if the alternative is playing sports, taking music lessons, painting, practicing for the talent show, or attending church youth group?

Psychologists agree that there are ways for teens to spend their free time that are just as healthy as, if not more so than, working a part-time job. And if the job is done solely so that the teen will have his or her own discretionary income, who is to say the money won't be spent on things unnecessary or even unhealthy?

I didn't want to get in the middle of the negotiations between my student and his boss. I did tell my student that if he decided to go on the mission trip, he could not expect his boss to change his mind and hire him back, nor could he be upset at a man who was simply trying to run his business as best as he saw fit. He decided to go on the trip, and it was life changing. And just as I suspected, the owner/church board member hired him back as soon as he returned. I believe God honored this student's openness and honesty about what he desired to do, and everything worked out.

I prefer this student's approach over another student, who bowed out of a different mission trip. She told me she had prayed about it and felt comfortable with her decision. Of course, we had already bought and paid for her ticket, and we had already guaranteed to the missionary how many students he could count on. Her comfort level included attending a wedding she wanted to go to and starting a job a little earlier that would pay her money. Her comfort became my discomfort.

In reflecting on a Christian work ethic, teenagers will often have to choose between what they want to do and what they have committed to do. Teens need to learn how to be open with their intentions while living by the golden rule, treating others the way they would want to be treated.

How do parents help their teens develop a healthy work ethic? Les Parrott III, in his book *Helping the Struggling Adolescent*, offers some guidance to parents and youth leaders in this area. The first thing the parent should do is assess the stress level. If the job is being done just to give the teen extra spending money and offers no gratification and is adding stress to his or her life, it isn't healthy.

Different jobs work for different teens. Some love flipping burgers; others like working in an office; still others would much rather be outside, working with their hands. Some teens are much better off not working at all, filling their time doing creative things that do not pay monetarily but add value to their lives.

If the job is being done just to give the teen extra spending money and offers no gratification and is adding stress to his or her life, it isn't healthy.

Help teens keep things in perspective. Because teenagers only have their limited view, they are prone to see problems at work or difficulties at school as be-all, end-all propositions. As a parent, you can help them step back and put school, work, family, and friends in a perspective that will hopefully help relieve some of the stress. You can also help them understand that God puts them in places for a reason. They won't be at this job forever, just like they won't be in school forever (it just seems like forever). While they are there, God can use them as his witnesses. This is why it is so important for teens to learn that in the workplace they treat people courteously, fairly, and give their bosses a full hour's work for a full hour's pay.

PARENT TIPS

1. ***It wouldn't be*** a bad idea to add up all the time your teen spends in a day doing the things he/she has to do and wants to do. Then decide with your teen if anything can be added or needs to go.
2. ***Having a job*** doesn't make teens mature; they are still teens working in an adult world.
3. ***Help teens*** budget their newfound riches by encouraging tithing to the church and insisting on saving some percentage of salary for long-term goals.
4. ***Don't forget*** to help teens see the difference between things they really need and things they want because they've seen them on TV or their friends have them.
5. ***Teens learn*** most of their work ethics, if not all, from their parents. If you work just to get, that translates very quickly to a teen that that is what work is all about.

Character Practices

For the Parent

- Think about your teen years. What were the ways you displayed a work ethic?
- Which word would you choose to describe your work ethic as a teenager: *weak, semi-strong, or strong?*
- Take time to think about your work ethic as an adult. What kind of example are you setting for your teenager?
- Consider one way you can help your teen understand the benefits of a healthy work ethic.

For the Couple

- Share with each other your concepts of work ethic.
- Based on your example as a couple, discuss how you think work is viewed by the members of your family.
- Take time to think about all the ways you are helping develop a work ethic within your teenager.
- Evaluate your work ethic as a couple. Discuss what needs to change, if anything.

For the Family

- Have a workday at home, where everyone is assigned certain tasks (laundry, mowing, leaf raking, and so on). To make it fun, have a pizza party at the end of the day. You may consider getting feedback about how members of the family felt about the day.
- Take your teen to work for a day. Let him/her see what you do and how you do it. If this is not possible, spend some time talking about what is involved at your place of employment.
- Go on a mission trip as a family. This could be a weeklong trip with your church or something you do in one day as a family.

Monday—Read Hebrews 4:1-13.

Begin to Think: On the seventh day God rested. He promises a rest for those who place their trust in Jesus. This is a rest that relies on the power of God in daily life rather than dependence on our human abilities. Those who place their complete faith and trust in Jesus enter this rest.

Begin to Talk: What is the rest that God provides those who follow him? How is the Word of God living and active?

Begin to Pray: That you would enter the rest God provides.

Tuesday—Read Hebrews 6:13-20.

Begin to Think: God made a promise to Abraham. In turn, Abraham waited patiently for God to fulfill that promise—God did what he promised. We can rely on the promises of God because he does not lie. The promises of God are like an anchor that keeps our lives safe and secure.

Begin to Talk: What are some of the promises of God? How are they like an anchor to our lives?

Begin to Pray: That you would place your hope in the promises of God.

Wednesday—Read Hebrews 10:1-18.

Begin to Think: Under the old law, atonement for sin was made through animal sacrifice. People sacrificed bulls and goats and offered them to God as a way of seeking forgiveness for their sins. These sacrifices were inadequate. Christ's death provided the ultimate sacrifice and permanent atonement for sin.

Begin to Talk: Why did Jesus willingly die on the cross? What should our response be to his sacrifice?

Begin to Pray: Thank God for sending his son to provide a way for the forgiveness of sin.

Thursday—Read Hebrews 10:19-39.

Begin to Think: Because of Jesus' death, we have direct access to the Father. He desires an intimate relationship with his creation. The only thing that can keep us from this close relationship is sin. In these verses, the writer gives the church the ingredients to persevering in our Christian walk and staying faithful to God.

Begin to Talk: What do you think it means to "draw near to God with a sincere heart"? How does the church (other believers) help us persevere in our faith?

Begin to Pray: That God would help you persevere in your faith.

Friday—Read Hebrews 11.

Begin to Think: There are many halls of fame (baseball, football, etc.). The writer gives a list of the heroes of the faith. Each one is unique and serves as an example of faithfulness to God. They are not superhuman; they are people like you and me who surrendered to the will of God.

Begin to Talk: What did you notice about each person mentioned? How can we strengthen our faith in God?

Begin to Pray: That God would strengthen your faith.

Once a year, as a youth pastor, I took my youth group to a nearby theme park (I don't remember the actual name of the place, but I think it was Six Flags over Purgatory). One of my favorite pastimes was to play mind games with 7th graders. So I got in line with a 7th grader for one of those death-defying, upside-down-looping, mega-g-force roller coasters. As we made our way through the line, I started my unnerving game.

I said, "They say this is the most dangerous roller coaster in the world." The young teen said nothing. I continued, "They say that sometimes people go out on the coaster, but they never come back." Again, the teenager just stood there saying nothing. I tried again, "They say that even if they come back, they are never the same." Silence from the 7th grader. And now I'm desperate because we're in the final leg of the line. I'm realizing that if I don't talk her out of riding soon, I'm going to end up on this killer coaster. My final shot, "You know, it's not too late. The exit is right over there. Leave now, and we can both be saved."

With that I could see the disgust in her eyes. That little 7th grader looked up at me and said in a clear voice, "You know, if you just trusted Jesus, I think you'd be okay."

That's not bad theology for a teenager. It is this sensitivity to the presence of Christ and his power that attracted me to youth work years ago. This new generation of young people needs very little proof that God is at work in their world. What they need help seeing is that God has a place for them in his story. Notice that I didn't say plan. The idea of God having a plan for teens today is too canned, too formulaic, too packaged, to have any meaning for their lives. What attracts them is an evolving story of God from Adam and Eve to Revelation.

Teens know that they also have a story. Their question would be, *Is there room for my little, insignificant story in God's big story?* The beauty of the answer is that not only does God have room for their stories; he wrote his story with them in mind. It's fun to be the youth leader, the Sunday school teacher, and certainly the parent who gets to share with a teen that among all the redemptive acts of God throughout history, their redemption is part of God's great story. God saving them through Christ is of no less importance to him than the Israelites passing through the Red Sea, Isaac being spared by God at Moriah, Gideon defeating the Midianites, or Paul's conversion on the Damascus road.

Teens also need space to discover what their belief in God really means to them. I taught college classes for a number of years. Occasionally I'd run into a straight-*A* student I really felt sorry for. Not because they didn't have a life. There are actually some *A* students who do have a life. I felt sorry for some of them because they had learned the content of the courses they were taking but didn't believe the content they had learned. They hadn't taken the time to think through what their answers meant. So even though they got most of the answers right, they had not allowed those answers to change them, mold them, or transform them.

Teens also need space to discover what their belief in God really means to them.

Teens need the time and space to be able to understand what their parents believe about God, Jesus, and the church and to figure out what that means to them. Their doubts, questions, and arguments can be frustrating; however, parents have to know that eventually their teens' faith has to be their own. As one person once put it, "God doesn't have any grandchildren."

This generation of teens is attracted to Jesus for different reasons than those who have gone before them. Jesus got down and dirty. He ate with sinners. He talked to the socially unacceptable. He challenged the rules. He suffered pain for other people's transgressions. It's this brokenness that teens today relate to so much. They are aware that the world is a cruel, tough place. They have been affected by broken relationships, hurt feelings, and injustice. If the wrongs of the world haven't affected them directly, they have friends who have suffered. To have a Savior who was wounded for them computes in their minds as one who not only relates to them but can indeed save them.

To take it one step further, if parents wanted to model a Jesus spirit for their kids, they would also have to be broken. This means that teens will follow the lead of their moms or dads spiritually when they see in them vulnerability and transparency that allow the teen to know that their parents are not perfect. Brennan Manning, author of *Abba's Child*, refers to these kinds of Christians as "wounded healers." These are people who work through the difficult times with God's help, and their faith grows in the process. For this generation of teenagers, wounded healers—parents who are not afraid to confess their doubts, fears, and hurts—will be most effective in translating what the gospel looks like in the home.

PARENT TIPS

1. ***Have a family*** prayer time with each member of the family, praying just one-sentence prayers, taking care to listen to the prayers of others who have prayed before.
2. ***Make a list*** of things you are concerned about as a family. This becomes your united prayer list.
3. ***As you read*** about and see the needs in your community, country, and the world, ask your family the question: What can we do as Christians to make a difference in these various needs?
4. ***In a quiet*** devotional time with the family, let each member write down on a piece of paper a word or phrase that represents a recent failure in their Christian lives. Then have each person fold their paper several times, put it in a container (like a tin can or outside grill), and, in the spirit of confession, burn the papers as a symbol of God's forgiveness.
5. ***As a family,*** visit each room in the house and pray God's blessing on all that goes on in those rooms. Pray for his protection, provision, and presence.

Character Practices

For the Parent

- Think back to your teen years. How would you describe your relationship with God?
- Take time to reflect on your relationship with your teenager. How comfortable are you with talking about spiritual things with your teen?
- Consider your relationship with God. What areas would you like to see strengthened?
- Make a list of five things you would like to see happen when it comes to the spiritual atmosphere in your home.

For the Couple

- Share with each other your thoughts and feelings about the spiritual environment in your home.
- Discuss the specific ways in which you nurture a spiritual sensitivity within the members of your family.
- Talk about ways in which you as a couple can model spiritual sensitivity more effectively.
- Decide on one thing you will do as an act of worship together as a family.

For the Family

- Set aside time this week to pray and read the Bible as a family.
- For the next month, after each Sunday service, take time to discuss the thoughts and feelings each family member had regarding the meaning of the morning message.
- Determine to increase the spiritual atmosphere in your home. This may be praying for your family out loud, talking about spiritual things, sharing your testimony, and so on.

Monday—Read Revelation 2:1-7.

Begin to Think: This letter is addressed to the church at Ephesus. Although they stand strong against evil and false teachers, they have forgotten their first love (for Christ and each other). They are to repent and go back to loving as they originally loved.

Begin to Talk: How do we keep our love for God and others from growing cold? What does it mean to repent?

Begin to Pray: That your love for God and others would not be abandoned.

Tuesday—Read Revelation 2:8-11.

Begin to Think: This letter is addressed to the church at Smyrna. Rather than a rebuke, the church receives encouragement. This church is facing persecution and poverty. The writer tells the church to remain faithful, even to the point of death. Those who overcome will gain eternal life with God.

Begin to Talk: What is an example of being persecuted for your faith? How do we stay faithful during times like these?

Begin to Pray: That you would remain faithful during difficult times.

Wednesday—Read Revelation 2:12-17.

Begin to Think: This letter is addressed to the church at Pergamum. The issue with this church is that there are those who are involved in idol worship and sexual immorality. The writer says that if they repent, they will receive spiritual nourishment from God.

Begin to Talk: What forms of idol worship exist today? In what ways do we express our worship of God?

Begin to Pray: That you would worship God only.

Thursday—Read Revelation 3:1-6.

Begin to Think: This letter is addressed to the church at Sardis. The issue is that this church is dead (in their faith). There are some who are faithful. Those who are dead need to repent. Those who are living faithfully will have their names written in the book of life (those who have accepted Christ).

Begin to Talk: How do we keep our faith alive? What do you imagine heaven to be like?

Begin to Pray: That your faith would be alive.

Friday—Read Revelation 3:7-22.

Begin to Think: These are letters written to the churches at Philadelphia and Laodicea. The church at Philadelphia is faithful and is told to hold onto their faith in Christ. The church at Laodicea, however, is lukewarm and doesn't even realize it. The writer tells this church to find their treasure in Christ rather than in earthly wealth.

Begin to Talk: What does it mean to be lukewarm? How do we listen to the voice of God in our lives?

Begin to Pray: That your life would be on fire for God.

30 TIPS FOR DEVELOPING HEALTHY CHARACTER WITHIN YOUR TEENAGER

1. Set a regular time each week to discuss what your teens are watching and listening to.
2. Familiarize yourself not only with the music your teens are listening to but also with the artists who sing the music.
3. Don't be too concerned with fads. By design, they are here today and gone tomorrow and usually reflect young people's need for identity.
4. Make sure your teens understand that computer filters and censors are in not in place because you do not trust them but are a protection from unscrupulous predators they would never suspect.
5. Teens should understand that purity is not perfection but a standard of honesty and morals that would be beyond reproach.
6. On the list of things you discuss as a family on a regular basis should be your stewardship of all resources.
7. One of the best things you can do as a family in the area of servanthood is support a child from Nazarene Compassionate Ministries. For about $25 a month, you and your family can feed and educate a child from a majority-world country and keep in regular contact with him or her.
8. Don't be discouraged if your teen doesn't get every lesson that could be learned from a service project. In God's good timing, he will use your teen's availability as a learning tool.
9. Don't forget to give God verbal credit in front of your children for what he has done.
10. It's a given that there are a number of things you do as a parent that are taken for granted. There are probably things teens do that go unmentioned too. It wouldn't be a bad idea to have a time to look each other in the face and say thank you for specific acts of love and service in the home.
11. True love allows parents to say "forgive me" when they are wrong. Don't hesitate to go further than saying you're sorry; ask to be forgiven.
12. Love involves eye contact and touching. Even if you are not a "touchy-feely" family, looking at your daughter when you talk to her and touching your son's shoulder as you pass by add points to your teen's emotional bank.
13. Your teens should hear how you've had to learn to love some seemingly unlovable people and what God has taught you about loving others.
14. A good exercise for your family would be to choose a people group you really don't know much about and maybe don't appreciate. The idea is to find information on this group, to discover what life is like for them, to understand how they think, and to learn why they do what they do.
15. Life is uncertain. Decide as a family that the last thing you will hear each other say as you say goodnight at bedtime is "I love you."
16. Explain to your teens that half-truths are as good as lies because they lead a person to assume something that is not true.
17. Be honest with your speech. If "I'll do my best" or "Let me think about it" have become code words for "I probably won't" or "No," then just say what you're really thinking and why.
18. Your teens need to know that you'll love them even if they lie to you, but they also need to know that there are consequences for their actions.
19. Just for fun, ask your teens if they think it is ever right to lie and see how they answer. As a parent, you really need to know what they're thinking about telling the truth.
20. It wouldn't be a bad idea to develop a family covenant of things each member of the family is committed to—whether it's never missing a sporting event or concert or eating breakfast together every Saturday morning.
21. It wouldn't be a bad idea to add up all the time your teen spends in a day doing the things he/she has to do and wants to do. Then decide with your teen if anything can be added or needs to go.
22. Having a job doesn't make teens mature; they are still teens working in an adult world.
23. Help teens budget their newfound riches by encouraging tithing to the church and insisting on saving some percentage of salary for long-term goals.
24. Don't forget to help teens see the difference between things they really need and things they want because they've seen them on TV or their friends have them.
25. Teens learn most of their work ethics, if not all, from their parents. If you work just to get, that translates very quickly to a teen that that is what work is all about.
26. Have a family prayer time with each member of the family, praying just one-sentence prayers, taking care to listen to the prayers of others who have prayed before.
27. Make a list of things you are concerned about as a family. This becomes your united prayer list.
28. As you read about and see the needs in your community, country, and the world, ask your family the question: *What can we do as Christians to make a difference in these various needs?*
29. In a quiet devotional time with the family, let each member write down on a piece of paper a word or phrase that represents a recent failure in their Christian lives. Then have each person fold their paper several times, put it in a container (like a tin can or outside grill), and, in the spirit of confession, burn the papers as a symbol of God's forgiveness.
30. As a family, visit each room in the house and pray God's blessing on all that goes on in those rooms. Pray for his protection, provision, and presence.

LEADER'S GUIDE

If you choose to use this as a small-group study, here are some tips to help you facilitate a group.

BEFORE YOUR FIRST SESSION

- **Give each person the student book one week prior to the first meeting. This will help parents prepare for the first session.**
- **Get an overview of each topic. This will help you:**
  1. Understand the direction of each lesson and the overall purpose of the study.
  2. Know what your parents will be reading.
  3. Begin to think and plan what you would like to accomplish by doing this study.

THE SESSIONS

Each lesson contains:

- **Parent Exchange**—time at the beginning of the session that allows parents to dialogue about what they are experiencing during this study.
- **Consider Life**—the introductory material relevant to the topic for the session.
- **Consider the Word**—the Bible study portion of the session.
- **Consider Your World**—the opportunity for parents to understand how the truth discovered during the session applies to their lives.

FLEXIBILITY

This material is designed to be studied weekly in 30- 45-minute sessions for 6 weeks. It can easily be adapted for different uses. You can study it on Sunday morning or evening and on weekdays.

Feel free not only to adjust the study to fit your needs but to customize each session to the group. Drop activities and discussion questions that won't work for you. Add others that will. Modify these lessons in the best way to fit your context.

ENCOURAGE EVERYONE

- *To reflect.* Invite them to reflect on the material prior to each session. This allows them to prepare their minds for the topic to be discussed that week.
- *To pray.* This allows them to prepare their hearts for what God wants to show them through the lesson.
- *To be open.* Be open to the lesson, the group members, and especially to God's leading.

1 SESSION

PURITY

Scripture Focus: Philippians 4:1-9

Bible Background: Paul urges the church to stand firm. He gives the followers keys to standing strong in the faith: agreement among believers, rejoicing despite the circumstances, gentleness toward all, and prayer. When followers of Christ have these elements working in their lives, their faith stands firm.

In verses 8-9, Paul talks about the importance of our thoughts. He is connecting our thoughts to our actions. Whatever is inside a person eventually is reflected in that person's actions. The beginning of a Christlike life begins with what's going on inside our hearts.

PARENT EXCHANGE

Divide your parents into small groups. Take a few minutes and invite parents to share about themselves (name, family, employment, and so on). After sufficient time, bring the group back together.

CONSIDER LIFE

Begin by asking your group members to think about what comes to their minds when they hear the word *purity*. Share with the group that purity does not mean perfect. It is a matter of the heart. Purity is "a condition of freedom from sin, of singleness of mind, of entire devotement to God."[3]

Follow up by asking:

- **Is having a pure heart and mind realistic? If so, how? If not, why?**
- **If purity is not perfection, what is it?**

CONSIDER THE WORD

Start the discussion by asking the group what it means to "stand firm in the Lord." After allowing time for several responses, read Philippians 4:1-9. Share with the group that in these verses Paul is saying "stand firm," regardless of what comes your way. He gives the church at Philippi those attitudes and actions that are important to a firm stance in our relationship with God.

Read verses 4-7 and ask:

- **How do our attitudes affect our actions?**
- **What role does prayer play in helping us "stand firm"?**
- **How does having God's peace guard our hearts and minds?**

Read verses 8-9 and ask:

- **Why should we think about things that are true, noble, right, pure, lovely, admirable, and praiseworthy?**
- **How do the things we think about affect the way we live?**

Then ask:

- **How could we apply these verses when it comes to living a pure life?**

CONSIDER YOUR WORLD

Purity is an ongoing process. Teens need to understand that there is no mathematical equation that can be used to equal a pure life. However, share with parents the following keys to helping them live with purity. Encourage parents to use these as talking points when discussing purity with their teenagers.

- ***Resist*** **anything that causes you to act and/or think in ways that are not pleasing to God. This might include magazines, websites, music, certain groups of people, movies, and so on.**
- ***Reflect*** **on things that are pleasing to God. Attitudes and thoughts eventually are revealed through your actions.**
- ***Remember*** **that God forgives and restores. If you sin, immediately confess it and ask God to forgive you.**
- ***Rely*** **on God's power and strength to help you. This is done through prayer, God's Word, and reliance on the Holy Spirit.**

---

3. Taylor, Richard S., ed. *Beacon Hill Dictionary of Theology* (Kansas City: Beacon Hill Press of Kansas City, 1983), p. 434.

2 SESSION

SERVANTHOOD

Scripture Focus: John 13:1-17

Bible Background: Near the time of the Passover feast, Jesus and his disciples gather for a meal. Jesus gets up from the meal and begins washing the disciples' feet. People wore sandals during this time period. As they walked, their feet became dusty. It was customary for the guests' feet to be washed upon arriving. This task was normally done by a house servant. Foot washing is a subservient act. For instance, a student would wash the feet of the teacher—but not the other way around.

Jesus, the Master, is washing the feet of his disciples. He is teaching them that serving God, serving others, and spreading the good news are what the kingdom is all about.

PARENT EXCHANGE

Divide your parents into small groups. Take a few minutes and invite parents to share what they discovered about purity from last week's lesson. After sufficient time, bring the group back together.

CONSIDER LIFE

Pass out a piece of paper and pencil to each person. Ask each person to write a word or image that describes the concept of servanthood. Allow time for people to think and write/draw. Then go around the room and invite each person to share their concepts. Follow up by asking:

- **Is servanthood something widely practiced in our world? Why or why not?**
- **Is servanthood something that comes naturally for people? If not, why?**
- **How do people develop a servant's heart?**

CONSIDER THE WORD

To begin, share with the group that Jesus and the disciples are sitting down for a meal. The time is just before the Passover feast. Jesus gets up, wraps a towel around his waist, and begins to wash the disciples' feet. The task of foot washing was done by servants or subordinates. For the Master to wash the students' feet was unthinkable.

Read John 13:1-17. Then ask:

- **How would you have reacted if you had been one of the disciples?**
- **Why do you think the disciples don't understand what Jesus is doing?**
- **What do you think Jesus is saying to Peter in verse 8?**
- **What is Jesus' message to the disciples in verses 14-17?**

Invite the group to reflect on the story for a few minutes. Follow up by asking,

- **From this story, what is Jesus' message to us today?**
- **How do we follow Jesus' example?**
- **What are the ways you can instill this message of servanthood within your teenagers?**

CONSIDER YOUR WORLD

Servanthood may be something that is more caught than taught. You must talk about it with your teens, but it is better learned through experiencing it in acts of service. While you cannot make your teens have a healthy idea of servanthood (or a servant's heart), you can do some things to help them experience service to others. Share the following ideas with your group:

- **As a family, volunteer at a homeless shelter, food bank, or clothing center. Don't make this just a one-time thing.**
- **Ask your pastor if there is anything your family could do to help others within the church.**
- **Look for opportunities to help others within your neighborhood.**
- **Determine to give a donation to a missions organization. Make it fun by raising the money through extra odd jobs, saving aluminum cans, and so on.**

Follow up by asking the group to brainstorm more ideas families can do to experience servanthood.

3 SESSION

LOVING OTHERS

Scripture Focus: 1 John 4:7-21

Bible Background: God is love. Those who love God must love others. The heavenly Father sent his Son to show us what true love is. Those who love God and have placed their faith in Christ have assurance of salvation and no reason to be afraid of God's judgment.

We who call ourselves followers of Jesus Christ must express love toward God and one another. If we claim to love God but do not love others, we are liars. The sign of God's love residing in a person's heart is his/her love expressed toward humankind. Christians do not live this life of love for God and others on their own strength but through the power of the Holy Spirit.

PARENT EXCHANGE

Divide your parents into small groups. Take a few minutes and invite them to share what they discovered about servanthood from last week's lesson. After sufficient time, bring the group back together.

CONSIDER LIFE

Begin by asking the group to think about ways a person could express God's love to the following individuals.

- *Homeless person*
- *Next-door neighbor*
- *Co-worker*
- *A person who cuts you off in the checkout line*
- *Someone who has spread gossip about you*
- *Your spouse (this would include an ex-spouse)*
- *Your teenager*

Follow up by asking:

- **When is it easy to express love toward someone?**
- **When is it difficult to express love toward someone?**

CONSIDER THE WORD

Begin by asking the group to think silently about how they would complete this statement: *I know God is love because . . .*

Follow up by reading 1 John 4:7-21.

Reread verses 7-12. Then ask:

- **Who is the "everyone" John refers to in verse 7?**
- **How did God demonstrate his love for us?**
- **What is the command in verse 11?**
- **Is it easier to love God (whom we have not seen) than it is to love others (whom we can see)? If so, why?**

Reread verses 13-15. Then ask:

- **According to verse 13, what does it mean to have God's Spirit?**
- **How does God's Spirit help us in our love toward God and others?**
- **How do we receive God's Spirit?**

Reread verses 16-21. Then ask:

- **What is the fear John is talking about in verse 18?**
- **How does God's love drive out this fear?**
- **How does saying we love God but not expressing love toward others make us liars?**
- **What is the command in verse 21?**

CONSIDER YOUR WORLD

Nurturing an attitude of love toward others within your teenagers begins at home. Teens must understand what it means to love God and to allow his love to flow through themselves toward others. This is not something that happens overnight but is a lifelong long process of learning and being led by the Holy Spirit. Share the following ways parents can begin modeling and teaching God's love within their families.

- As a parent, take time to share with your family what you have learned over the years about God, his love, and what it means to love others.
- Become more comfortable with saying "I'm sorry" and "I forgive you."
- As a family, make a conscious effort to say "I love you" more often to members of your family.
- Make a plan, as a family, to do one selfless act for someone outside your household during the course of the next week.

Close in prayer, asking the Holy Spirit to give you the strength and power to love as God loves.

INTEGRITY

4 SESSION

Scripture Focus: Matthew 5:33-37

Bible Background: An oath is something where your words signify a promise made to someone. During the time of Jesus, oaths were very common. The Old Testament teachings (Exodus 20:7; Leviticus 19:12; Numbers 30:2; Deuteronomy 5:11; 6:13; 23:21-23) made it clear that people were to keep their word. However, many religious leaders had discovered ways in which to get around keeping the oaths they made.

Jesus said not to make an oath but to let your "yes" be "yes" and your "no" be "no." That is to say, let your words be truthful and trustworthy. A person's word is nothing unless it is backed up with a life of integrity.

PARENT EXCHANGE

Divide your parents into small groups. Take a few minutes and invite them to share what they discovered about loving others from last week's lesson. After sufficient time, bring the group back together.

CONSIDER LIFE

Begin by asking your group to respond to the following scenarios.

- *Bill is out of vacation days at work. He would like to take Friday off and is thinking about calling in sick that day. What advice would you give Bill?*
- *You overhear your teenager boast to a new friend that he/she knows karate. You know that your teen has only been taking karate for a month. What might you say to your teen about this conversation?*
- *A friend has just bought a new car. You absolutely dislike this make and model of vehicle and have heard many bad things about the performance level of this particular type of car. Your friend tells you how much they like the car and asks your opinion about his/her purchase. How would you respond?*

CONSIDER THE WORD

An oath is a ***solemn promise:*** *a formal or legally binding pledge to do something such as tell the truth in a court of law, made formally and often naming God or a loved one as a witness.*[4] Share with the group that oaths were common in the days of Jesus. Some religious leaders had discovered ways in which to get around keeping their oaths. They worded oaths in such ways as to give themselves loopholes in having to be bound by their promises.

Read Matthew 5:33-37. Then ask:

- **What is Jesus saying about making oaths?**
- **What is involved in making an oath?**
- **Does placing our hands on the Bible, crossing our hearts with our fingers, or saying "I promise" make our words more truthful? If not, why?**
- **What does it mean to let our "yes" be "yes" and our "no" be "no"?**
- **To whom are we accountable for the words we speak?**
- **How does truthfulness build healthy relationships with others?**
- **If you were asked to paraphrase these verses, what would you say?**

CONSIDER YOUR WORLD

Share with the group that the writer to the Hebrews says in 13:18, "Pray for us. We are sure that we have a clear conscience and desire to live honorably in every way." Honesty and integrity are as much a matter of the heart as they are a matter of our words and actions.

Close by reading the following practical ways to practice honesty for parents to share with their teenagers.

- *Be conscious of the things you say.* Are you in the habit of saying things that are less than truthful?
- *Confess wrongdoing and ask forgiveness.*
- *Keep promises.* If you say something, back it up. If you can't back it up, don't promise it.
- *Determine in your heart to be truthful.* Ask the Holy Spirit to guide your thoughts and words. Spend time in God's Word and discover what it means to live with integrity.

---

4. <http://www.bing.com/Dictionary/search?q=define+oath&FORM=DTPDIA&qpvt=oath+definition>. Accessed March 7, 2011.

5 SESSION

WORK ETHIC

Scripture Focus: Ephesians 4:28; 6:7; Colossians 3:23; 1 Thessalonians 4:11-12

Bible Background: Work is a part of life. We work for food, shelter, and clothing. We work to buy the things we want in life. Some people have a positive view of work, and some have a negative view. Some people have a good work ethic (belief in the value of hard work), and others do not.

God intended for his creation to work. We see this in the garden of Eden. Adam is given the instruction to work the garden and name the animals (Genesis 1:27-30; 2:15-20). Throughout the Bible, we read passages that instruct us on how to view and approach work.

PARENT EXCHANGE

Divide your parents into small groups. Take a few minutes and invite them to share what they discovered about integrity from last week's lesson. After sufficient time, bring the group back together.

CONSIDER LIFE

Begin by asking the group to respond, true or false, to the following statements. Be sure to take time between each statement for people to explain their responses.

- **A good work ethic is something that comes naturally for most people.**
- **Most people view work as a means to buy food, shelter, and clothing.**
- **Christians should have a different view of work than those outside the faith.**
- **Our view of work should encompass every aspect of life, rather than just apply to our place of employment.**
- **The Bible has little to say about work.**

CONSIDER THE WORD

Share with the group that Christians should have a biblical view of work. From this biblical viewpoint comes our work ethic. Read each of the following Scripture passages.

"Anyone who has been stealing must steal no longer, but must work, doing something useful with their own hands, that they may have something to share with those in need." —*Ephesians 4:28*

Ask:

- **Why is it important for people to work and be productive?**
- **Should work just be about being able to buy the things we need or want?**

"Serve wholeheartedly, as if you were serving the Lord, not people." —*Ephesians 6:7*

Ask:

- **What does it mean to work wholeheartedly?**
- **How does this apply inside and outside the church?**

"Whatever you do, work at it with all your heart, as working for the Lord, not for human masters." —*Colossians 3:23*

Ask:

- **How does this verse help us in our view of work?**
- **What does this mean for our relationships with our bosses and coworkers?**

". . . and to make it your ambition to lead a quiet life: You should mind your own business and work with your hands, just as we told you, so that your daily life may win the respect of outsiders and so that you will not be dependent on anybody. —*1 Thessalonians 4:11-12*

Ask:

- **What is the benefit of a strong work ethic for us?**
- **How does having a positive work ethic benefit others?**

CONSIDER YOUR WORLD

Share the following for parents to use when talking with their teenagers about the advantages of developing a strong work ethic.

- **Self-sufficiency.** Work makes it possible for people to rely on themselves rather than others.
- **Independence.** Those who are self-sufficient are independent.
- **Fulfillment.** Give your best and work hard, and you will feel fulfilled.
- **Self-esteem.** Being a hard worker and giving your best will build confidence and self-worth.
- **Charity.** The goal of working should not be to buy, buy, buy, but to use it for good and to help others.